Kicking Ass
and
Taking Names

Kicking Ass
and
Taking Names

Paul Allen Payne

outskirts
press

Kicking Ass and Taking Names
All Rights Reserved.
Copyright © 2019 Paul Allen Payne
v2.0

The opinions expressed in this manuscript are solely the opinions of the author and do not represent the opinions or thoughts of the publisher. The author has represented and warranted full ownership and/or legal right to publish all the materials in this book.

This book may not be reproduced, transmitted, or stored in whole or in part by any means, including graphic, electronic, or mechanical without the express written consent of the publisher except in the case of brief quotations embodied in critical articles and reviews.

Outskirts Press, Inc.
http://www.outskirtspress.com

Paperback ISBN: 978-1-9772-1221-4
Hardback ISBN: 978-1-9772-1410-2

Outskirts Press and the "OP" logo are trademarks belonging to Outskirts Press, Inc.

PRINTED IN THE UNITED STATES OF AMERICA

Dedication

*This book is dedicated to my three
daughters, Cynthia, Angela and Meredith. It
is also dedicated to my five grandchildren,
Trey, Seth, Grace, Owen and Lily.*

*They all serve as a daily reminder that
life's most precious gift is family.*

*And, to my wife, Mary, my life partner
and best friend for almost fifty years.*

*We've experienced a tremendous journey
together, and look forward to what lies ahead.*

Table of Contents

Chapter One 1
   There Can't Be a Tree Left
   Standing in Tennessee

Chapter Two 9
   How NOT to Fire Someone
   (The James Comey Story)

Chapter Three 17
   I'm Not Firing You . . . You
   just Fired Yourself

Chapter Four 27
   The First Time Someone Kicked My Ass

ChapterFive 35
   Be Still, My "Unused," Achy Breaky Heart

Chapter Six 45
   My 280-Year Career in
   Human Resources

Chapter Seven 53
    The Inmates Are Running the Asylum

Chapter Eight 61
    Better Hiring Means Less Firing

Chapter Nine 69
    Careful Folks . . . It's a
    Minefield Out There

Chapter Ten 81
    Treat Everyone Fairly . . . With
    Kindness, Dignity, and Respect

Introduction

During my 40-year career in HR, I have probably been involved in hiring and firing more people than Donald Trump. After several years of relating many hair-raising and outrageous stories to my wife, she told me I ought to write a book. So, here we are. Everything in this book is true . . . Yes, it all actually happened. In all instances, the names have been changed to protect the innocent, or the guilty, as the case may be.

I can honestly state that I have never been involved in firing anyone who didn't deserve to be fired. I can also state that I have been involved with hiring some folks who, in retrospect, should never have been hired. But, that is where the firing part comes in because in many instances, we end up having to fire our hiring mistakes.

Let me stress that throughout my career, I have found that 90–95 percent of all employees are there to work hard and do a good job. It's that 5–10 percent of the workforce who seemed intent on making my life miserable.

CHAPTER ONE

There Can't Be a Tree Left Standing in Tennessee

My career in HR began in a carpet manufacturing plant in Northwest Georgia many years ago. I knew absolutely nothing about Human Resources Management (or Personnel Management, as it was called back then). I began my employment there as a management trainee in the Management Training Program. It was a fairly loosely structured program (compared to those of today), but it gave the participants an opportunity to learn the entire carpet manufacturing process. We would spend time in the various departments, learning how all the manufacturing processes worked and were coordinated with all the other departments in each step of the manufacturing process.

Seeing a roll of carpet being made is a pretty interesting thing to observe. We would often have visitors come into the plant, just off of I-75, and they would want to observe the process. One of the things contained in the job description for a management trainee is being a tour guide for all the visitors who stopped in, wanting to see how carpet is made. I often thought . . . *Don't these people have somewhere they need to be?* It was usually an entire family with kids, and I'm thinking, *OK, here's a bunch of kids on their way to Florida, anxious to get to the beaches, and they're stopping in for an hour to tour a smelly carpet manufacturing plant.* But the kids were generally pretty attentive and asked probing questions about the process, such as, "How many breaks do the workers get?" and "How long do they last?"

The parents always seemed very interested in observing the process. After all, you get to see a giant sewing machine with over 1,000 needles sewing yarn into a jute backing. Following this, the roll of sewn jute and yarn is transported to the Dye Department where the roll is fed into giant dye vats, for coloring the yarn. Afterward, the roll is then transported to the Coating Department where a secondary layer of jute backing is coated onto the roll of jute and yarn with a latex adhesive, thereby locking the yarn tufts into place. Once this is completed, you have a finished roll of carpet.

There Can't Be a Tree Left Standing in Tennessee

The plant ran three shifts per day, sometimes 6 or 7 days per week. Back then, we were producing about 20 miles of carpet per day. I'm not sure what the capacity is like today, but if it is like most manufacturing productivity in America, I suspect that it is now well beyond that level of production.

My management trainee position eventually led me to a position in the "Personnel Department" (aka HR Department). The trainee positions were designed to set up a "pipeline" of management talent to be trained in all facets of carpet manufacturing and then have the candidates slotted into management positions as the opportunities arose. In my particular situation, the Assistant Personnel Manager had just left the organization, and I was asked by the Personnel Manager if this was an area that I would be interested in.

Having just spent the month of August driving a Hyster, loading rolls of finished carpet into the giant tractor trailer trucks for shipment all over the U.S., in 90-degree heat with no air-conditioning, the thought of a cool office setting sounded appealing. So, I said, yes. As a matter of fact, at this point in my management training program, I would've said yes to a position of sharpening pencils for the secretarial staff, if it got me into an air-conditioned office.

The Assistant Personnel Manager job proved to be quite interesting and challenging. The biggest challenge for the Personnel Department was keeping this huge carpet mill staffed in order to run 24 hours per day, sometimes 7 days per week (depending on the demand for carpet at the time).

We had over 1,000 employees at this facility, and employee turnover was a continuous problem. Most of the jobs in the mill were hot and sometimes strenuous (i.e., see above referenced Hyster driver job). Very few of them required a lot of experience, so we hired lots of folks with no experience and trained them on the job. I spent the bulk of my time interviewing and hiring candidates for these entry-level positions.

There Can't Be a Tree Left Standing in Tennessee

We tried to put a lot of emphasis on hiring candidates with good, stable work records. Of course, this was not always possible. Our county bordered on the Tennessee state line, and we often had candidates come down from Tennessee looking for work in our plant. I began noticing a trend during my early interviewing days. It seemed that the vast majority of candidates coming in would state on their application that their job for the past 5–7 years had been cutting pulp wood for their uncle in Tennessee. Of course, how are you supposed to verify this work history? A call to Uncle Clem in Cleveland, Tennessee, would verify that, indeed, his nephew Bubba had worked for him for the past 5 to 7 years (fill in the blanks) and that "He was the best employee that he had ever had."

Well, what do you know . . . Of course, he was.

No offense to the good folks of Tennessee, but just . . . damn!

After many years of hiring lots of these folks from Tennessee, and I must admit that most of them were pretty good workers, I finally came to the conclusion that there can't be a tree left standing in Tennessee!

CHAPTER TWO

How NOT to Fire Someone
(The James Comey Story)

If ever there was a true-life, high-profile case study on how *not* to fire someone, this is it. We all saw it unfold right before our very eyes a couple of years ago when the former head of the FBI, James Comey, was fired.

As I recall the events, Comey had flown in the FBI private jet to California and was making a presentation to a group when it was announced on TV that Comey had been fired. So, basically, Comey learned that he had been fired when the rest of America was hearing that he had been fired. Of course, there had been days of speculation prior to the actual firing that this may, or may not, be happening soon. What struck me about the entire event was how poorly it was handled. When I first heard about it, I thought, no, I'm sure the president had met with him and explained that his services were no longer needed in the Trump administration.

But, as it turned out, that was *not* how it happened. The event turned out to be a public spectacle and embarrassment and humiliation for Comey.

If only Trump had allowed him to finish his presentation in California and called and told Comey he wanted to meet with him in the Oval Office the next morning . . . There, he could have held a private conversation with Comey, letting him know that his services were no longer needed in his administration. He could have told Comey that he was willing to allow him to resign, and that Comey could then publicly announce that he was resigning to pursue other opportunities. This would have helped to save face for Comey and still achieved the president's objective of removing him from this powerful public office. Just think how much grief this could have saved President Trump . . .

Instead, Comey had a personal vendetta to get back at Trump for all the public humiliation caused by how his firing was handled. Hell, I've seen Trump use more compassion when firing Meat Loaf on his reality TV show, *Celebrity Apprentice*.

And what about poor Omarosa? He had to fire her twice, once from *Celebrity Apprentice*, and the second time from her cushy White House job, whatever that was. (I'm not sure anyone ever figured out what she was doing there.) And just like Comey, she went on to write a book about it, and just as Comey did, probably made tons of money off it, all the while gleefully slamming Trump.

What seems to be overlooked in the Comey firing is that his position serves at the pleasure of the president. Trump could have told Comey he didn't like the cheap ties he was wearing from off the rack at JC Penney's and fired him for that. (Particularly since they weren't coming from the Donald Trump Collection at $200 a pop.) The bottom line is this . . . Whenever you're firing someone, the process *has* to be handled professionally—with dignity and respect for the person being fired. After all, you are about to drastically change this person's life, affect their source of income, and deliver a blow to their sense of confidence and self-esteem.

Anytime you can turn a firing situation into a scenario where you first allow the person to resign to pursue other opportunities, it can become a win/win for you and the person being fired.

You achieve the same result, the person is leaving your workforce, and they are permitted to leave with some modicum of dignity in hand. But always allow them to put into writing their written resignation. Give them a copy and keep a copy for the Personnel File.

In some instances, the employee will refuse to resign and state that, "You're going to have to fire me." *That* is when you kick their ass and take their name.

I used to worry a lot about what the employee would do or might do after they were fired. Only one time during my entire career that I know about did a fired employee go home and commit suicide. This bothered me greatly throughout my career, and it served to reinforce my practice of always treating the employees with dignity and respect. It also showed me that some things are out of my control.

How NOT to Fire Someone(The James Comey Story)

We continue to hear about workplace violence and shootings within the workplace. These often involve a recently fired employee and usually a manager, HR manager, or coworker. You have to wonder how the firing was handled, and could the outcome have been avoided if the situation had been handled differently?

Fortunately, I have never encountered any workplace violence such as this during my career. However, I was "invited" out to the parking lot once, by an employee who had just been fired. But, that is a story for later in the book, which I will describe in some detail.

CHAPTER THREE

I'm Not Firing You . . . You just Fired Yourself

When it comes time for the firing event to take place, it is rarely a surprise for the soon-to-be-ex-employee. Particularly if the manager of the employee has done a proper job of notifying the employee of their deficient performance and properly documented the Personnel File for the record. Under a typical company's Rules of Conduct, outlined in the *Employee Handbook*, there exists a Progressive Disciplinary Process. This lays out for the employee the types of misconduct that are unacceptable within the workplace and what actions will be taken if the rules are infracted. Usually, the Progressive Disciplinary Process is a three-to-four-step process that should occur before the actual firing takes place. The process typically goes something like this:

Step One/First Offense: Verbal Counseling (although it is only verbal counseling, the conversation needs to be documented for the file, dated, and signed by the manager and the employee). There is an old adage in personnel parlance that is as true today as it was 40 years ago, and it goes something like this . . .

"If it doesn't get documented for the file, then it never happened." Just try walking into an Unemployment Hearing with no documentation in the Personnel File and explaining to the Unemployment Hearing Officer why you just fired this employee. The situation basically becomes your word against the employee's, and in my experience, the Hearing Officer will rule in favor of the employee every time. They tend to take a dim view of employers who do not follow the steps in their own Progressive Disciplinary Process.

Step Two/Second Offense: Written Counseling, which documents the event or events that took place which warrants the Written Counseling. It should also be notated what the next step will be if there is a recurrence of this problem.

Step Three/Third Offense: Final Warning. This step places the employee on final notice that if there is any further infraction of this Rule of Conduct, then the employee will be terminated.

Some employers may choose to offer a fourth step in their Progressive Disciplinary Process. This may consist of a 3-day suspension without pay, or sometimes, it is referred to as a Decision-Making Leave, without pay, for 3 days. During this final step process, the employee is instructed to go home for 3 days and make a decision about whether they are able to return to the work setting and abide by the rules. If they decide that they are not able to return to work and abide by the rules, then we will accept their resignation at that time. If they decide to return to work, then they are given one last opportunity to become a productive employee and conform to the Rules of Conduct. However, if there is another rules infraction within a specified period of time, typically 3 to 6 months, then the A.K. commences. (I realize that the term "Ass Kicking" can be viewed as a harsh term, so going forward, I will refer to it as "A.K.")

Over the years, I've encountered some employees who try to turn this into a game. They will infract the rules right up to the limit and somehow, miraculously, decide to conform to the rules until their time-framed counseling sessions expire, thus giving them a clean slate to begin the process all over again, or so they think. There comes a time when you have to invoke the "Cumulative Effect" Rule. That is, when you assess the overall performance of the employee over a period of time and determine that the employee has accumulated so many rule violations that they are determined to be more of a liability to the organization than an asset. The manager is having to spend an inordinate amount of time managing the employee's performance and is at the stage of pulling out hair, gnashing teeth, and wringing hands. This is when the manager will typically come to visit with the HR Director and state that they are at their wit's end, the employee is driving them crazy, and what can be done to hasten the exit of this derelict employee from the organization.

Typically when the manager arrives in that state, there has been another incident, which, for lack of a better HR technical term, is known as the "Last Straw." This is when it is time to sit with the manager, review the employee's Personnel

File in its entirety, and create a chronological list of all the infractions which have taken place over the course of the employee's work history with the organization. Generally, when I have sat with managers in this situation and reviewed the totality of the infractions, I often ask, "Why didn't you fire this employee a long time ago?" And you know . . . I have never heard a good answer to that question. That is when we move to the A.K. phase.

A majority of the time, when an employee is shown their chronological list of infractions and told we are giving them an opportunity to resign right now or be fired, their response is . . . Where do I sign?

Over the years, I have encountered employees whom I suspected wanted to be fired. I have also suspected a number of reasons for that. Probably at the top of the list would be that they wanted to quit working and start drawing Unemployment Insurance Benefits.

After all, you get paid, yet you don't have to work. However, there is a minor detail about Unemployment Insurance Benefits some may not be aware of . . . You can only receive the benefits if you have lost the job through "no fault of your own." If the employer has properly followed its Progressive Disciplinary Process and documented the Personnel File accordingly, chances are pretty slim that the employee will be allowed to receive the Unemployment Benefits. However, if the file has not been properly documented in accordance with what the Progressive Disciplinary Process calls for, then get out the checkbook, because this ex-employee is about to "get paid."

During an Unemployment Hearing, if you are unable to produce the written documents that led to the firing, then the Hearing Officer will side with the fired employee. Remember the aforementioned HR Rule #1: *If it doesn't get documented for the file, then it never happened.* So write it down, damn it!

So, back to my original premise, if these steps are followed with the employee, there are no surprises when the employee is called to the manager's office or HR Dept. for the final time. You didn't fire them; they fired themselves.

CHAPTER FOUR

The First Time Someone Kicked My Ass

If you live long enough and work long enough, eventually, you are probably going to be fired from a job at one time or another. It happens to the best of us *and* the worst of us. It just seems to happen to some folks more than others. It has happened to me during my 50-year work history, and it was a very painful and humbling experience. (My first 10 years of work consisted of delivering newspapers, bagging groceries, and various construction jobs.)

I once heard Rush Limbaugh say that he had been fired eight or nine times. He went on to say that he had actually lost count, given the fact that it had happened so often. For those of you who might know who Rush Limbaugh is, you'd have to agree that things have worked out pretty well for him. For those of you who don't know who Rush Limbaugh is, just Google his name, and you'll find all you need to know about him. Last time I looked, he was making about $85 million per year and carries a net worth of about $500 million (not bad for a college dropout who has been fired from that many jobs).

My point in writing this chapter is to emphasize that there is no shame in being fired from a job. For some, as it did for me, it opens up a lot of possibilities that you might not have ever recognized or realized, had you stayed in the same job for your entire career.

My Dad worked for the same company for 40 years. I always marveled at how he was able to get up each day and go off to work with a smile on his face and do essentially the same job, day after day, year after year. To my knowledge, he never missed a day of work in those 40 years, except at the end when he was diagnosed with lung cancer and died 6 weeks later. I sometimes wished that he had left that job and gone and explored some other opportunities, but he always seemed happy and content in doing what he was doing, and I guess, in the end, that is all that really matters.

*****

One day, during an otherwise routine workday at the carpet mill, where I hired and fired employees, I was invited to fisticuffs out in the parking lot. Now, *that* is a way to liven up an afternoon at work.

The aggrieved employee had been fired the previous day and was back demanding his paycheck. This scenario actually happened quite often during my career. The Georgia State law calls for a fired employee to be paid their due wages on the next scheduled payday. This law varies by state, with some state laws requiring you to pay the fired employee their due wages at the time they are fired.

As it turns out, this employee was fired on Wednesday, and the regularly scheduled payday was every Friday. He showed up in my office and demanded that he be paid his due wages. I explained to him that all wages are paid on Friday. He stated in no uncertain terms that he wasn't leaving until he received his paycheck that was due him. I further explained that he was not getting paid until Friday, so he was apparently in for quite a wait. At this suggestion, he became further irate and invited me out to the parking lot where he stated that he would take the wages he was due "out of my ass."

Being one to never back down from a fight, this invitation raised my ire considerably. I stood up from my desk and looked out my window into the parking lot. There was his pickup truck near the entrance with three other "gentlemen" sitting in the front seat waiting for him. Back then, all the pickups only had one-row seating, so, no matter how many passengers you had, they all had to ride in the front seat. Unless, of course, you had the overflow crowd riding in the bed of the truck (which wasn't an uncommon sight in North Georgia during those days, prior to the advent of two-row seating in pickup trucks).

We had a saying at the time that "More than three people in the front seat of a pickup truck looks tacky."

So, as I assessed the tacky crowd waiting for me at the front door, I declined his offer to "step outside" and courteously reminded him that he could pick up his check on Friday.

The First Time Someone Kicked My Ass

He turned and left without further incident, and that was the last I saw of him. Oh well, back to the desk and figuring out who needs to be hired and/or fired next.

To help quantify the scope of the challenge in keeping a 1,000-plus employee carpet mill staffed, with a 40–50 percent turnover rate, we needed to hire 400–500 employees every year just to keep the place running. (Thank God for all those pulp wood cutters from Tennessee!)

*****

It was a cold day in mid-December in North Georgia when I informed my boss that I needed to leave early that afternoon to attend my grandmother's funeral. He stated that I didn't need to worry about leaving early because I was being fired that day.

I won't go into the details about why I was fired because you probably would not believe it anyway. Suffice it to say that I was treated incredibly unfairly, and to this day, I have used the experience as a stepping-stone and impetus to move forward with my life.

Getting fired enabled me to return to college and complete my undergraduate degree. I also completed my law degree following this unfortunate episode in my life.

I made a vow never to allow an unfair situation like this to happen to me and my family again. I also vowed never to allow a circumstance like this to happen to any employee in any work setting over which I had any control.

CHAPTER FIVE

Be Still, My "Unused," Achy Breaky Heart

There is an old joke that has been around the HR business for years. When I first heard it, I thought that it was a good joke and that it clearly captured the essence of what working in HR was all about . . . until I heard the joke's punchline, that is.

The joke goes something like this . . .

Two employees who were fired by the same company ran across each other one day while standing in the unemployment line, and one said to the other . . . "You know, if I ever need a heart transplant, I hope I can receive one from an HR Director." "Oh, and why is that?" inquired the other ex-employee. "Well," he replied, "if it comes from an HR Director, then we can be assured that the thing has never been used."

I must admit that this stung a bit after I first heard it, but then I was able to rationalize and interpret the real meaning of the so-called joke. When working in HR, and it comes time for the really tough decision of whether to fire an employee, the decision must be made with your head and not your heart. If all the firing decisions were made with the heart, then no one would ever get fired. Just think about it . . . I'm sure that if all disciplinary measures were meted out by the heart, they would probably go something like this:

"OK, Ruppert, if you miss one more day of work this month, in addition to the 8 days you've already missed, I'll be forced to place you in time-out for 30 minutes." (Of course, this time will be spent in the employee break room, where all the vending machines and coffeepots are located.) Or maybe something like this . . . "Maggie, you were observed on the company's security camera piercing your supervisor's tires with what appeared to be an icepick. We're not certain because the video was somewhat grainy, so, maybe it was only a nail file. Nonetheless, you will be required to report to the Employee Training Room and write 50 times on the grease board . . . 'I will never deflate my supervisor's tires again with an icepick or nail file.'" I think you get the picture . . . Without strict rule enforcement,

Be Still, My "Unused," Achy Breaky Heart

you soon have the inmates running the asylum. (More to be said about that later in the book.)

The bottom line is this . . . If you're going to be an HR Manager or in any management position, for that matter, you've got to grow a backbone. You have to be willing and able to make the tough decisions when it comes to disciplining an employee. It is never easy, and I don't think I've ever heard anyone say that it was. As a matter of fact, many managers have confided in me that they consider this aspect of their job to be the toughest part.

I can probably count on one hand the number of managers I have worked with over the years who seemed to almost relish being able to fire an employee. Quite frankly, this small group of managers has always concerned me greatly.

I could never bring myself to relish firing anyone, except just once, and when I share the story with you, you will have to admit that you probably wish you could have been a fly on the wall for that one.

During my 40-year career in HR management, I have worked in three different industries: health care (i.e., hospitals), manufacturing (i.e., making rugs), and financial services (i.e., banking). I found that people are basically the same, regardless of the industry, and all the HR principles apply across industry lines.

Of the three industries, I always considered health care to be the most challenging of the bunch. The diverse mix of people in a hospital setting makes for some very challenging, yet interesting times. You're dealing with everyone from doctors to nurses to volunteer staffs, and all the different positions in between. The last time I counted, there were well over 100 different positions that made up a hospital workforce.

This particular situation I am about to describe involved a registered nurse. He was a male RN and had been on the job for about 5 years. He worked on a post-surgery floor and was responsible for administering medications to patients who had just undergone surgery.

He had been considered to be a good nurse over the years and had gotten good employee evaluations and raises to recognize his good performance.

During his last days of employment with us, some of his patients began to complain that they were experiencing more pain than they felt like they should be during their post-surgery recovery period. We discussed this situation with him, and, of course, he denied any involvement with this problem and stated that he did not know what could be happening. The problem continued, so, we set up security surveillance cameras in the room where the medications were being prepared for administration to the patients. There, his scheme was discovered. He had been diverting some of the pain medication from the syringe and filling it back up with water. Therefore, the patients were getting maybe half the dosage their doctor had prescribed, while he was keeping the other half for his own use.

When we confronted him with the video evidence, he fully confessed to what he had been doing.

Of course, he was terminated on the spot for being a thief (i.e., stealing hospital drugs) but also for a far worse reason; he was depriving innocent patients of their proper dosage of pain control medications. I can't think of a more despicable thing to do to someone or a more despicable human being who would do such a thing.

Some might ask, did you refer him to a drug rehab program for help with his addiction? The only referral we made was a criminal referral for being a thief and otherwise low-down, dirty, rotten scoundrel.

The justice he deserved and received was a perp walk out the front door of the hospital wearing a pair of handcuffs.

The last I heard about this individual was about 2 years after he was fired. I saw a brief blurb in the local newspaper stating that he had died of a drug overdose. The article did not state whether it was determined to be a case of suicide.

But you know, that Karma thing can be a real bitch sometimes.

CHAPTER SIX

My 280-Year Career in Human Resources

When I began my career in HR in the early 1970s, the position did not hold anywhere near the power or prestige that it does today. It has been great to watch how the position has grown in its importance to the organization over the years.

Early on, I once heard the Personnel Department referred to as the "Attic of the Industry." The meaning being that anytime there was a task to be performed that no other department wanted to do, the simple solution was to "let Personnel handle it." As a result, a lot of less-than-desirable things (i.e., crap) ended up as functions of the Personnel Dept., or in other words, being sent to the "attic."

Some days, working in the HR Dept. could be likened to that of a dog's life. As you are probably aware, a dog ages at seven times the rate of a human. So, when a dog turns 1 year old, he is actually 7. When he turns 10, he is 70. You get the picture. (Hence, 40 x 7= 280 years I spent working in the Personnel/Human Resources/Attic of the Industry).

The part that ages you the most in working in HR is when you have to "lay off" an employee. This is when the employee loses their job through no fault of their own. It generally is caused by a downturn in the economy when the work orders are not there in order to keep a plant running at full steam.

Layoffs also come when one company buys another, and you have overlapping geographic regions and duplication of services. So, naturally, you end up closing some facilities and keeping others. (This happened quite often while I worked in banking. I called it the "Pacman Effect.")

This is, without a doubt, the toughest part of the HR function, and there have been times when I'm not sure that the 7 times multiple is an adequate number to calculate the toll that it takes on you as part of the aging process.

*****

One of my favorite HR success stories involves the now-retired former CEO of Delta

Airlines, Ron Allen. Ron worked for a number of years as the head of HR at Delta Airlines. I'm not quite sure what they called the position there, because the title varies greatly from one company to another. I've seen the title range from executive vice president of Human Resources to Head People Person.

Anyway, back to the Ron Allen Story. The day Ron was promoted to Delta's CEO was a particularly exciting day for everyone working in an HR position. It gave us all hope that maybe one day, our career path might take us from HRD to CEO. (Perhaps Ron tired of the pressure-packed HR role and yearned for the easy life in the executive suite . . . Just kidding, Ron; you inspired us all.)

While working in the hospital industry, I was privileged to meet many talented HR Directors from across the state of Georgia. One of my proudest moments came when I was elected president of the Georgia Society of Hospital Human Resources Directors. In this role, you get to know many of the HR Directors pretty well, as we met often and exchanged ideas and best practices with each other. We had over 100 members in this organization, and it became quite interesting to learn of the varied backgrounds of the HR Directors from across the state. One particular characteristic I found among several of the HR Directors was that they were retired military officers and were beginning their "second" careers as hospital HR Directors. There is a saying that, "Old soldiers never die, they just fade away." This led me to conclude that "Old soldiers never die . . ." They just retire and become HR Directors at hospitals (and as I recall, based on the feedback I used to receive about them and my interactions with them, they were all quite good at their jobs).

The typical HR Department today will usually handle about five primary functions that they are responsible for at their company. These are: Recruitment (Hiring), Employee Relations (Firing), Wage and Salary Administration, Training and Education, and Employee Safety. Of course, these may vary with each different organization, but these make up the main functions.

It's the add-ons and miscellaneous functions that have sometimes led the HRDs to drink. In some instances, you are almost like a cruise director on a ship, making sure that everyone is having a great time on their "journey." You almost need a full-time event planner to get through it all. And who knows, maybe there is such a person now in some HR Departments.

You've got the Service Awards Banquet, the employee picnic, the employee Christmas party, the Easter party, the St. Patrick's Day party, the Fourth of July party, the Labor Day party, etc. (You get the idea.) Also, there are committees to be formed and meetings to be held to discuss each of these events, along with another committee to plan what other events we need to add to the list of observances that may have been overlooked, heaven forbid.

I had heard that one of my seasoned colleagues from across town was retiring after a rather lengthy career in HR. I called him to wish him well in his retirement, and he stated (and this is verbatim) . . . "Yeah, I was afraid that if I had to plan another Service Awards Banquet that I was going to get in a tower and hurt someone."

Luckily, last I heard, he had retired peacefully to a farm way out in the country, away from the maddening crowd.

CHAPTER SEVEN

# The Inmates Are Running the Asylum

There is a strange phenomenon that can occur whenever a group of employees are not properly managed. Without proper guidance and certain levels of conduct expected, employees may develop a misguided perception that they are in charge of running the organization.

I have witnessed this in several work settings during my HR management consulting practice. It is a fairly ugly sight to behold and generally requires some strict management intervention in order to restore order to what is usually a chaotic situation.

Let's face it . . . Some people just aren't cut out to be managers. Some find themselves thrown into a manager's role without proper preparation or training. In some instances, the person tapped to be the manager is the one who has been the most technically proficient or the most skilled in their particular job.

Becoming skilled at managing people is *usually* a long and arduous process, requiring many months of formal training sessions, covering many varied topics on how to effectively manage people. I use the word *usually* because I have seen exceptions to this rule on many occasions. I've seen those who are natural leaders and are ready to be put in charge with a minimum of management training courses. While at the other end of the spectrum, I've worked with those who are just not meant to manage people. It takes a certain skill set, some of which I think is innate, in order to be an effective manager of people. Some are just not successful as managers, regardless of the number of management training courses they may have attended.

Training to be an effective manager of people is an ongoing, career-long process. Throughout my career, I have taught many management training courses, but also, I have probably attended about as many as I have taught.

You know something, managers get their tails kicked just like the rank-and-file staff do. Ineffective managers have to be dealt with in a strict manner, else it can bring down the entire organization. Of course, they are given the same disciplinary process as is afforded all employees within the organization. Managers are also graded on very different criteria than the regular employee. Managers may be graded on such things as: employee turnover within their department; meeting productivity standards; employee opinion survey data; meeting departmental budget numbers . . . And the list goes on and on.

Most employers these days are very metrics-driven and have very quantifiable goals set for their respective management team members. These goals are usually discussed and agreed upon between the different levels of management at the time they are being set. As a result, they become part of the Manager's Performance Review Process and help decide how the manager is graded out at the appropriate Performance Review interval. These too can vary greatly by company. I have seen some Performance Review sessions done on a quarterly basis, some on an annual basis, but it certainly ought to be done at least once per year, preferably more often than that.

While working in the health-care industry, I had an opportunity to consult with and advise many hospital CEOs on how to handle their "people problems." These were the things that they seemed to need the most counsel with, except for one particular CEO. He had a way of dealing with his deficiently performing managers, which I thought was particularly effective, and it always seemed to produce the desired result. And the amazing part was, he never had to "fire" any of them.

Here's how it worked. Of course, they were all given their Quarterly Performance Reviews based on the mutually agreed upon metrics criteria that drove the performance of the respective manager's department. After several quarters of not meeting the standards that were set for the department, and after some very straight talk about the underperforming department and the consequences that were impending, the final discussion went something like this . . . "Well, we can do this the '*hard way*' or the '*easy way*,' and I'm going to let you decide which one you choose." The "*hard way*" consisted of going on a strict month-to-month probationary period for the next 90 days, during which time the metrics would be evaluated at the end of each month, and if an agreed upon number was not met, then the manager would be fired.

Or, the "*easy way*" allowed the manager to voluntarily resign and spend the next 30 days looking for a job while remaining on the payroll.

During my many years of working with this CEO, I never saw a manager choose the "*hard way.*"

In fact, all those who left the organization seemed to truly appreciate the opportunity to "resign" to "pursue other opportunities."

CHAPTER EIGHT

Better Hiring Means Less Firing

I've always felt that if we did a better job screening and selecting candidates on the front end that we would do a lot less firing on the back end. But that has always been easier said than done.

After all, hiring an employee is a very inexact science. A lot of the hiring decision is based on your gut instincts about the candidate after all the interviews have been done, and the references have been checked. (This part is becoming more and more difficult, as most employers are sharing less information about past employees.) But you have to make the best decision you can make based on the information you have.

Most of the hiring decisions I have made have been based on the actual face-to-face interview with the candidate. I still believe this to be the best method for selecting the best candidates.

Interviewing methods have been improved over the years as the illegal, discriminatory-type questions have all been eliminated (hopefully, for your employer's sake), and behavior-based questions have become the gold standard for today's best interviewing technique.

Just to illustrate how far the questioning has evolved over the past several decades, I can recall employment applications having such questions as: "Where do you attend church?" "Where were you born?" "When were you born?"

Behavioral interviewing questions probe into certain job-related behaviors such as: "Tell me about one of your most recent work projects you were involved in, and what the outcome was." "Tell me about a time when you were most frustrated at work, and what you did to overcome the frustration."

Hearing answers from questions such as this can tell you a lot about a candidate, and this is just for starters. Typically, an employment interview will last anywhere from 30 minutes to an hour.

Forty-five minutes is a good average time for an interview. This will allow enough time to get acquainted with the candidate, and then have an in-depth discussion on maybe eight to ten pertinent behavioral interviewing questions.

My recruitment trips over the years have taken me to many interesting places. My employers always placed a heavy emphasis on college recruiting. Some of the best recruiting trips have been to Duke, Emory, Tulane, Stetson, Alabama, Florida, and Georgia. (Go Dawgs!)

There have been many memorable moments recruiting at these schools, and we have hired several good employees from each of them. One particular instance comes to mind that I will share with you. One of my favorite questions to ask during on-campus interviews has been the following: "What do you consider to be your most significant accomplishment during your 4 years here at _____ University?" (I am purposely leaving the name of the school blank, so as not to embarrass any of the alumni from this school.)

As you might imagine, after several years of on-campus recruiting at many different schools, I have heard lots of very interesting answers to this question.

Typically, the responses will be something like, "I am most proud of the fact that I was on the Dean's List for three semesters during my time here, and I ended up with a GPA of 3.75."

Others would be something like . . . "I was able to complete all 4 years with no student debt, as I held a part-time job all through school, usually working 20–30 hours per week."

But the following answer was my favorite . . . After having posed the question, you just sit back and listen in silence as the interviewee formulates his or her thoughts. As any good interviewer will tell you, just let the silence continue, because the ball is in the candidate's court, and you are expecting an answer, sooner or later.

After about a full minute of complete silence, along with some fidgeting and looks of despair, the candidate responded: "The thing I am most proud of during my 4 years here is that I have never missed a home football game."

OK, I know this response helps to narrow down the field of schools from which the answer came, as it was obviously one of the SEC football schools named previously. But I will assure you that it did not come from *my* alma mater. (Go Dawgs!)

Needless to say, this candidate did *not* receive an invitation for an on-site visit to our organization. However, I feel certain that he probably landed somewhere on his feet. At least, he exhibited two very good traits, which are loyalty and dedication to his team, and these are admirable qualities to possess. (Just don't mention this answer to an interviewer when you are trying to land your first job out of college!)

CHAPTER NINE

Careful Folks . . . It's a Minefield Out There

Working in HR is a career choice fraught with legal peril. Many times, when an employee is fired, their first thought is . . . "I'm going to sue this place for what you've done to me!" Boy, if only I had a nickel for every time I've heard that one!

I once thought about getting one of those little number dispensing machines (the ones you see in the bakeries). The plan was to set it up on the corner of my desk, and when the recently fired employee threatened to sue, I would point to the machine and tell them to "take a number and get in line." I thought it was a cute idea, but as I gave it more thought, I determined that it was probably not one of my better ideas. Some folks might not be in the proper state of mind to appreciate the humor about that device, so I abandoned the idea.

I did, however, retain my "No Whining" sign and prominently displayed it on my desk for several years, until one day, it struck me . . . This thing isn't working. I continued hearing a constant stream of "whining" coming through my office. (Particularly after someone had just been fired . . . Guess there was some cause and effect there.)

*****

Some Thoughts about Sexual Harassment . . .

We in the HR Department have a "duty to act" whenever a complaint is made to our department concerning an allegation of sexual harassment. During my many years of handling these complaints, I have found that the complaint is very credible in about 99 percent of all cases. But then there is that 1 percent that is not credible, and those are the ones that are particularly difficult to ferret out.

My experience has shown me that it takes a lot of courage to come forward and file a complaint of sexual harassment against one of your coworkers, or even more so, against your boss.

Sexual harassment can have a fairly wide-ranging meaning, but it is generally construed to be "any unwelcome or inappropriate physical or verbal behavior of a sexual nature." The severity of the offense is usually dependent upon how pervasive the conduct is. Once a complaint is filed, it is incumbent upon the HR Department to take swift, remedial action regarding the complaint.

My approach in handling these situations was that they always become my top priority because each case is always to be taken seriously, regardless of who is involved and no matter how serious or frivolous the circumstances may sound.

And here is where the courageous part comes in . . . A charge of sexual harassment cannot be made from the shadows or done anonymously. The complainant was always required to put their complaint in writing, detailing specifics of the charge, along with dates, times, and places. They were also required to sign and date their written statement. Most of these cases come down to "he said, she said," as there are rarely any witnesses to this type of activity.

However, if the complainant had any witnesses, then they are interviewed, and a signed statement is taken from them as well. Following this, the alleged harasser is called in for an interview and told of the allegations against him or her. The responses I have heard range from stunned silence to "Yeah, I did all those things, but I was just kidding around."

Just as was the case many years ago, there remains today a vast ignorance over what constitutes sexual harassment in the workplace and what type of conduct is—or isn't—acceptable.

A good number of employers today have initiated sexual harassment training for their employees and managers. This is a step in the right direction, though the subject seems to stay at the forefront on the nightly news, as many high-profile cases continue to make the news on a fairly regular basis. (E.g., Matt Lauer, Bill Cosby, Charlie Rose, etc.)

Every case involving alleged sexual harassment has to be investigated thoroughly, and the action to be taken depends on the severity and pervasiveness of the circumstances. Many times, the complainant has come into my office and stated . . . "Look, I don't want anything bad to happen to this person, I just want them to stop bothering me." This seems like a reasonable request, though whether "anything bad" is about to happen to the harasser is now out of the accuser's hands and up to the outcome of the investigation.

Some situations have been resolved with a "written warning" being placed in the Personnel File, while others may lead to immediate termination.

A Case in Point: While working in banking, I once had a young teller come to my office to complain that one of our customer service employees had asked her out to the movies on several occasions, and she had repeatedly told him no. As it turns out, she was single, and he was married with four children. The teller was aware of his marital and parental status and informed him that she did not date married men.

When he was invited in to give his version of the story, he said, "Yeah, I did ask her several times. I just like to go to the movies." At this point, I had to ask . . . "OK, how does this thing work? You load up your wife and four kids in the car and then stop by and pick her up?" This is when the stunned silence sets in. As we concluded the meeting, we both agreed he would not be asking this teller to anymore movies. A "written warning" was placed in his Personnel File, and we never had another problem with him.

It is also very important to let the accuser know that the employee has been dealt with, and that if there are any other issues that may arise concerning this individual, to let the HR Dept. know immediately.

Another Case in Point: While working in the hospital, a nurse came into my office and complained that when she was in the Operating Room with this particular doctor, he would pinch her on the rear end every time he walked behind her. Now, these situations become a little more difficult, because, technically, these doctors are not our employees. However, they are using "our Operating Room" at "our hospital" and therefore, must conform to the rules that govern conduct within our work setting. In most hospital settings where the doctors are not employees of the hospital, their allegations of misconduct against them are handled by a Medical Review Board, or some other committee the docs assign to investigate such matters among themselves, which consists of other doctors who are on the medical staff at the hospital.

In this particular instance, we were given assurance by the chairman of the Medical Review Board that appropriate action had been taken against the physician, and this was then communicated to the nurse. She was also told if there were any other instances involving this doctor, that she should report this to the HR Dept. immediately.

One other point I should make about doctors who are not employees of the hospital. They are eligible to be sued by the hospital employee for sexual harassment. The doctors may also be held liable for monetary damages payable to the employee. Many physicians have been held liable for damages ranging up to a million dollars or more for their improper conduct within the hospital setting.

We periodically scheduled Sexual Harassment Training for the medical staff. During this training, we reviewed actual cases where doctors were held liable for monetary damages to the hospital employees due to sexual harassment.

During my many years of working in the hospital industry, this was the best way of getting the "full attention" of a doctor that I have ever witnessed.

> A few thoughts about Hostile Work
> Environments and Retaliation . . .

Another facet of sexual harassment is the aspect of creating a hostile work environment. This can be done without any physical abuse but is generally verbal in nature. Things such as sexually suggestive remarks, sexually suggestive photos in the workplace, or off-color jokes can be considered harassment if they are considered intimidating, hostile, or offensive to a reasonable person.

Retaliation against an employee who has made a complaint against a coworker or manager or doctor can have dire consequences for the one who retaliates against an employee. If you, as a manager, decide to retaliate against an employee who has filed a sexual harassment complaint against you, buck up, because I can assure you, you are *not* going to like what happens next. Bye-bye.

CHAPTER TEN

Treat Everyone Fairly
. . . With Kindness,
Dignity, and Respect

Throughout my entire career, I have operated off of a basic premise, which was as follows: Treat people the way you would like to be treated. Or, put into more recognizable biblical terms, it is the Golden Rule, which states . . . "Do unto others as you would have them do unto you."

This simple yet profound statement has served me well during my career, as well as throughout my entire life.

I have always been regarded as a rather quiet, reserved person who was perceived by most people as being "nice." This persona almost cost me a promotion once and here is why: During my "Pacman" years in banking (i.e., the bigger banks gobbling up the smaller banks), I worked at a smaller banking company that was acquired by a larger bank. The usual "musical chairs" of management positions ensued. A regional HR Director position was available, and I told the state HR Director that I would like to be considered for the position. So, I "threw my hat into the ring." During my formal interview for the position, I was told by the state HR Director that he wasn't sure I was "mean enough" for the position. I remember thinking . . . *Gee, maybe I should have him speak with my three teenage daughters, who, at this particular time, probably thought I was the meanest person on the planet. After all, they had an 11:00 p.m. curfew, when all their friends had to be home by midnight.* My constant retort whenever I was challenged by one of my daughters about this "harsh" and "unreasonable" time was, "There is nothing going on after 11 p.m. that you need to be involved in." This brilliant quip usually shut down any debate, though many nights I could hear mutterings underneath their breath as they sauntered off to their room.

While this may have been considered harsh at the time, it is a particularly prideful moment for a parent when he learns that his daughters are now using this same line on their own children who are now in their teens. (The legacy lives on . . . smile.)

The Pickle Predicament…

I was reminded by one of my daughters recently that I was so mean when she was growing up that she wasn't allowed to have an extra pickle on her Chick-Fil-A Sandwich.

Gee, the last time we were together in a car going through the drive-thru at Chick-Fil-A must have been 30 years ago. I guess I didn't realize that I had scarred her for life. Though she related this story in a joking manner, I could still see the hurt in her eyes as she conveyed this story to the entire family during a recent visit.

Please allow me to explain this situation from my perspective, so as not to come off as quite the ogre as I have been depicted.

As you are probably aware, the Chick-Fil-A drive-thru lines move pretty quickly, as they have always been the model for how to move cars efficiently through a drive-thru line. Anyway, as we would enter the line, the chirping would begin from the three in the backseat, and it usually went something like this . . . "I want extra pickles on my sandwich" . . . followed by another voice chirping . . . "I want extra mayonnaise on my sandwich" . . . followed by another voice chirping . . . "I don't want any pickles or mayonnaise on my sandwich" . . . so . . . By the time I got to the "squawk box" (i.e., order microphone), I was so confused I didn't know what to order, and I certainly didn't want to slow down the fast-moving line.

My order usually sounded something like this . . . "Give me five Chick-Fil-A sandwiches, and that will be all."

Of course, this was met by a chorus coming from the backseat of "Daaadd!!!"

The standard Chick-Fil-A sandwich comes with a piece of chicken and a pickle. (Mayonnaise packets are thrown in, if you ask politely.)

My usual reply to the peanut gallery in the backseat was . . . "OK, you in the back who didn't want any pickles, give it to your sister who wanted an extra pickle." Also, "You wanting the mayo, I'm pretty sure we have a jar of mayonnaise at home, and I can hook you up."

Since we lived 3 minutes from the restaurant, I was pretty sure that the sandwich wouldn't be spoiled by the time we got home for lack of mayonnaise. "Oh, and for you who didn't want any mayonnaise on yours . . . be sure and not put any on it when you get home." I always liked to end our exchanges with a little humor, but I don't recall hearing much laughter coming from the backseat . . . particularly after our visits to Chick-Fil-A.

Anyway, back to the interview for the regional HR Director position, I did not tell him to speak to my daughters; instead, I told him, "Do not mistake my kindness for weakness," as I was able to make the tough decisions whenever the situation called for it, though I never considered it as being "mean." My style could better be characterized as being "firm but fair, with a smattering of treating everyone with kindness, dignity, and respect." (By the way, I got a call a week later and was given the promotion to Regional HR Director)

*****

A Policy to Ensure Fairness in the Workplace . . .

I want to share a tool with you that serves to ensure that there is always fair treatment for everyone in the workplace, be it employees or management. This tool involves a process that is laid out explicitly whenever a new employee joins the company, and it is there for them to access if and when they feel that they have been treated unfairly in the workplace. Many companies have such a process, and it can be called many different things. Some call it a Grievance Procedure; some call it a Fair Treatment Process. It really doesn't matter what it is called as long as it is available to all employees whenever it may be needed, and that it is administered fairly and in accordance with its prescribed guidelines.

It's a fairly simple and straight forward process, and I have seen it work well over many years of administering the program during my role as HR Director.

It goes something like this . . .

Step One: Submit any problem, concern, or dispute to your immediate supervisor. Hopefully, the issue can be resolved at this level, and that is the end of the problem.

Step Two: If your supervisor does not resolve the issue to your satisfaction, then you may appeal this decision to the department director. The department director will then meet with the employee and the supervisor, and after a review and investigation of all the facts in the case, a decision is then made by the department director.

Step Three: If the response from the department director does not resolve the issue or complaint of the employee, then that decision may be appealed to the executive management of the facility.

Step Four: If the response from the executive management does not resolve the issue to the satisfaction of the employee, then this decision is appealed to a committee. The committee consists of five employees from the company, three of whom are non-management employees, and two who are management employees. These selections are made randomly by the employee and HR representative.

Once the committee is convened, the process moves fairly quickly. The aggrieved employee presents his or her case to the committee. Witnesses may also be used if they have relevant firsthand information concerning the case.

(I should interject here that most of the cases that reach this stage in the process involve an employee who has been fired, and they do not think it is fair.)

After the aggrieved employee has presented his or her case, the employee's manager then presents the case as to why the employee was fired and presents the relevant documents for the committee to review. If the manager has followed the proper disciplinary procedures as outlined in the *Employee Handbook*, the committee will generally agree that the firing was justified and will affirm the termination. The decision is made by a vote of the committee. The decision rests with the majority of the committee's vote. A 3 to 2 vote decides the outcome. The committee is purposely made up of an uneven number, so there is never a tie. It's just like the Supreme Court and their nine members. There is never a tie.

Step Five: If the aggrieved employee does not accept the decision of the committee, then that individual may appeal their case to the final step in the process, which involves Final and Binding Arbitration. This involves submitting the case to an arbitrator for a final and binding decision of the case.

After having handled dozens upon dozens of these cases over the years, I could count the number of cases that have gone to arbitration on one hand. The committee process is generally the last step utilized by most employees. There is something about having your case reviewed and decided upon by a group of your peers and a couple of folks from management that leads the employee to believe that they have been given a fair shake. They've had an opportunity to "state their case," to "have their day in court," and most are accepting of this decision, be it for or against them (and in most cases, the decision is against them).

The fact that most cases are not won by the employee during this process has always been an affirmation that the supervisors and managers in the workplace are treating their employees fairly, with kindness, dignity, and respect. But it has also been very reassuring to know that this process is in place for the employee to access at any time it is felt to be necessary.

Treat Everyone Fairly...With Kindness, Dignity, and Respect

This "tool" is always emphasized during the New Employee Orientation to the company. It is spelled out clearly in the *Employee Handbook*, which each employee receives during the orientation process. A "Handbook Receipt" is also signed by the new employee during orientation, and a copy of the receipt goes into their Personnel File. The receipt states that the employee was given a copy of the handbook, which contains the Rules and Regulations which govern the conduct of employees at the company, and that they are expected to familiarize themselves with these policies and conduct themselves accordingly while employees at this company.

This handbook is a "must-have" for all companies and HR departments. If your company doesn't have one, contact me. I know a guy.

Summary

I've always had a keen sense of fairness and justice. The only times I can recall ever being told that I was being unfair was when my daughters were going through the 3- or 4-year-old stage, and whenever they were being punished for something, their standard complaint was "That's not fair!" Well, my standard reply was, "Oh yes, it is . . . Your sisters did the same thing once, and they received the same punishment, so, that makes it fair." Boy, talk about a way to shut down an argument with a 3-year-old. As they were rendered speechless after this pearl of wisdom, they would then retire to the corner of their room, sucking their thumbs, and finally understanding what the word "fair" means.

Throughout my career, I do not recall anyone ever leaving my office sucking their thumb, nor do I recall anyone leaving my office claiming they had been treated unfairly.

As unpleasant as it is to have to mete out discipline to an employee, as long as it is done with kindness and compassion, most rational people will understand the necessity of the action and accept it as being "fair treatment" for their act or acts of indiscretion.

It all comes down to trying to always "do the right thing" for whatever the situation calls for.

A bank president I worked with for several years once told me that I had the ability to tell someone to "go to hell," and by the time the conversation was over, they were looking forward to the trip. I didn't know quite how to take this initially, but I think there was a compliment in there somewhere. It has to do with always leaving the employee with hope and optimism for the future. My conversations usually ended with wishing the employees "good luck" for their future and telling them to feel free to contact me if there were ever anything I could do to assist them, in any way.

Through the years, I have actually had a few ex-employees call and thank me for the kick in the rear end that they received. They went on to tell me how the experience had changed them—for the better—and enabled them to take the situation and use it as a learning experience.

It is very gratifying to receive an occasional call from someone who got their career start following our meeting at a Career Fair or college recruitment interview and have gone on to have successful careers.

These are the rewards that have made a life-time career in Human Resources seem worthwhile.

The End

Special Thanks

I want to offer a special thanks to my granddaughter, Grace. She spent a good portion of her Summer transcribing my manuscript into its typewritten form, from handwritten chicken scratch on a yellow legal pad.

Also, a special thanks goes out to my grandson, Owen. He offered some much needed technical computer support while working with me this Summer on the farm.

www.ingramcontent.com/pod-product-compliance
Lightning Source LLC
Chambersburg PA
CBHW031437210526
45464CB00005B/2240